Whoopies!

Whoopies!

52 seasonal mix-and-match
recipes for whoopies

Susanna Tee

NH

NEW HOLLAND

Contents

Introduction

A cupcake please... No, make that a whoopie!

So, what's the secret? How does a delicious delicacy that has only been sampled by the chosen few suddenly become a global trend? Certainly, in the case of the whoopie or whoopie pie, that is exactly what seems to have happened. One moment, cupcakes had the big city bakery shelves all to themselves; and the next, the whoopie pie had turned up like a forgotten country cousin and muscled in on the action. Perhaps those regions of the United States where whoopies have long been a traditional treat decided they'd kept their secret long enough. Maybe the whoopie just needed to find its way to the fashionable bakeries for word to spread. What is not in question is that everywhere from New York's Magnolia Bakery to Harrod's in London, and many bakeries sandwiched in between, the whoopie is winning new fans.

The recipes in this book capture some of those things that might lie behind the whoopie's success. There are simple options for the basic whoopie that might be considered more manly than your average cupcake. Then there is a dazzling variety of cakes and fillings, so that you can discover the true versatility of the whoopie. For whoopies as fancy as the prettiest cupcake, you will discover how to add glacé icing or roll your whoopie in delicious decorations. Children will love to help decorate them, and to clean the bowl. The recipes are grouped by the four seasons so that you can enjoy the freshest local ingredients when choosing which ones to make next. There are also ideas for presenting your whoopies for special occasions, and templates for gift boxes. So, what's the secret of the whoopie's success? Read on, and find out.

Whoopie
Doo

A Short History of Whoopies

A whoopie pie, a whoopie cake, or do you call it a whoopie cookie?

Not only is the name of the whoopie unclear, but its origins are also uncertain. The whoopie would probably be declared the official dessert of the Maine in the US if such a thing existed, but Boston and Pennsylvania also claim the honour of being its birthplace.

There are Mainers who will testify that they were weaned on whoopies. One theory is that whoopies were introduced to Maine when a woman working in a commercial bakery baked some leftover cake mixture instead of wasting it, and put it together with some extra filling. From this, the whoopie was born.

The Boston claim is through a recipe leaflet, first published in 1930 by the Durkee Mower Company, called The Yummy Book. The company is the manufacturer of Marshmallow Fluff, which is used as a whoopie filling. The Yummy Book is still in print and has been updated many times, although a recipe for whoopies didn't appear in the publication until the 1970s.

Food historians, however, believe that it was the Amish women living in the Pennsylvania region who created the whoopie. Whoopies are certainly part of their culture and they are sold at all Amish markets, farmers' markets, road-side stands offering baked goods, gas stations and convenience stores. One view is that the origins of the whoopie lie in medieval Germany, and when the Amish settled in Pennsylvania in the nineteenth century, they brought the whoopie with them. Another unproven notion is that Amish women baked leftover cake mixture and put the resulting pies in their husband's and children's lunch boxes. On opening and finding the goodies, the latter shouted 'Whoopie!' for joy.

Whatever its name or origins, the whoopie is the perfect easy-to-make, fun-to-eat treat for any occasion. This cookbook has a year's worth of sweet recipes sandwiched between its covers, and as the song writer Gus Kahn wrote for the 1928 Broadway musical *Whoopee!*:

Another season, another reason, for makin' whoopee

Or, in this case, whoopies! So, simply delve into these pages to find a collection of delectable recipes. Whoopie!

Below: **Amish workers carrying their lunch boxes out to the fields seem to suspect that the man on the right has been lucky enough to have a whoopie packed.**

Equipment & Ingredients

A large bowl, a free-standing mixer or a hand-held electric mixer, several large baking sheets, baking paper, a wooden spoon, a tablespoon, palette knife, sieve and wire rack are all you need. A whoopie pan, an ice cream scoop and a piping bag with a large star nozzle are useful.

The whoopies can be baked on large baking sheets (keeping the batter well apart to allow for spreading). I have found that the sheets worked best when lined with baking paper instead of being greased. Alternatively, you can use a whoopie pan, which has 12 shallow wells, and these should be greased.

Spooning the whoopie mixture onto the baking sheets or into the wells of the pan with a tablespoon, using a finger to slide it off the spoon, is the traditional way, but using an ice cream scoop creates uniform shapes. Choose one that measures 5 cm/2 inches in diameter.

A sieve is necessary to incorporate the dry ingredients evenly into the mixture, and a wire rack is needed to allow the whoopies to cool without becoming soggy underneath. Once baked, the whoopies need to be left for only a minute or two on the sheets or in the whoopie pan to allow them to settle before transferring them to a wire rack.

COOKERY NOTES
- This book uses both metric and imperial measurements. Follow the same units of measurements throughout; do not mix metric and imperial.
- All spoon measurements are level. Teaspoons are assumed to be 5 ml and tablespoons 15 ml.
- Recipes using raw egg whites should be avoided by infants, the elderly, pregnant women, convalescents and anyone with a chronic illness.
- Unless otherwise stated, milk is assumed to be full fat, eggs are large and individual fruits are medium sized.
- Pregnant and breast-feeding women are advised to avoid eating peanuts and peanut products.

The basic ingredients for whoopies are flour, a raising agent, salt, sugar, egg, a milk product (usually buttermilk) or milk, a fat and a flavouring, very often vanilla, which, in fact, brings out the flavour in chocolate whoopies. Traditionalists consider that whoopies should only be chocolate flavoured, but these days flavourings vary.

The best-risen whoopies are those that use plain flour and baking powder, but whoopies are traditionally baked with buttermilk, which nowadays replaces naturally soured milk, and this acid ingredient needs bicarbonate of soda (an alkali) to balance the acid to alkali ratio.

Granulated sugar is also a traditional ingredient, but caster sugar can be used instead. Soft brown sugar, either light or dark, is equally suitable, adding colour and flavour to the whoopies and making them slightly moister.

Large eggs have been used in the recipes and ideally should be removed from the refrigerator before using to let them come to room temperature. This prevents the mixture from curdling, but it isn't essential so don't worry if you forget.

The recipes in this book use butter, because most households will already have it in the refrigerator. However, there is no reason why you can't replace all or part of the butter with vegetable shortening if you prefer. Vegetable oil is also sometimes used.

Traditional fillings include Marshmallow Fluff, the original commercially produced marshmallow crème. Other marshmallow crèmes have a thinner consistency and you may need to add a little more sugar to thicken them.

Hints for Perfect Whoopies

While making whoopies is pretty simple and you're probably debating which recipe to make first, take a few moments to read through these few secrets that I have discovered on my quest to bake the perfect whoopie.

• Before you do anything, preheat the oven.

• Measure the ingredients accurately and use the correct measuring spoons.

• Don't overmix the mixture; stir gently until the ingredients are just combined. There are several reasons for this: overmixing will cause the mixture to peak in the oven and have a tight, compact texture, resulting in a tough whoopie without that melt-in-the-mouth quality.

• It's fine to leave the mixture to rest for 5 minutes on the baking sheets or in the pan before baking, but don't leave it any longer because, in the case of baking powder, once liquid has been added to it, it will start to activate.

• Try to resist the temptation to open the oven door during baking, but be vigilant towards the end of the cooking time, as the whoopies can change colour in a minute or two.

• Oven temperatures vary and we tend to know our own ovens. I suggest that if you are baking several sheets of whoopies at once, instead of rotating them during cooking, it is best to bake the top sheet for about 10 minutes, remove it from the oven and then move the bottom sheet up a shelf and bake for an extra 2–3 minutes.

Filling Whoopies

When the whoopies are cold, match each whoopie half with its closest partner in size. The filling can then be spread onto the whoopies with a palette knife or knife, but it looks more attractive when swirled on using a piping bag fitted with a large star nozzle.

The best way to fill a piping bag is to put a large star nozzle in the end and then stand the bag in a jug or tall tumbler and fold back the top of the bag. Spoon the filling into the bag and turn down the top. Only fill it halfway up the bag, because otherwise when you pipe the mixture, it will come out the wrong end.

To pipe the mixture, put the nozzle of the filled bag close to the whoopie and, holding the bag in one hand and supporting it underneath with your other hand, squeeze the bag firmly to push out the icing. When you have finished, lift the bag sharply off the cake and you will have a beautifully filled whoopie.

How to Store Whoopies

As a batch of baked whoopies usually makes about 12, you may want to know how to store them. They can be stored in an airtight container in a single layer or stacked, with the layers separated with baking paper. Alternatively, wrap them individually in clingfilm. They will keep at room temperature for up to three days, if any should happen not to have been eaten before then.

Whoopies can also be packed in an airtight freezer container or wrapped individually, undecorated, and stored in the freezer. Thaw at room temperature for 2–3 hours before serving.

How to Eat a Whoopie

When it comes to eating, you will be aware that some of the generous filling is lost out of the sides. When this happens, open it, collect up the filling that has oozed out with a finger, put it back onto the bottom half and then recreate the whoopie – only to do it all over again a few bites later. This is the correct way to eat a whoopie.

Spring

Classic Whoopies

Makes 12

115 g/4 oz butter, softened,
   plus extra for greasing
200 g/7 oz soft dark brown
   sugar
1 tsp vanilla extract
1 large egg
280 g/10 oz white plain flour
50 g/1¾ oz cocoa powder
1¼ tsp bicarbonate of soda
pinch of salt
225 ml/8 fl oz buttermilk

Filling

Home-made Marshmallow
   Crème (see page 75)
   or Classic Marshmallow
   Filling (see page 73)

This is the traditional whoopie recipe, featuring a chocolate cake mixture similar to that other great classic, the rich, dark devil's food cake, filled with Home-made Marshmallow Crème.

1 Preheat the oven to 190°C/170°C fan/375°F/Gas Mark 5. Line 3–4 large baking sheets with baking paper or grease the wells of a whoopie pan.

2 Put the butter, sugar and vanilla extract in an electric mixer bowl, or use a large mixing bowl and a hand-held electric mixer, and whisk together until light and fluffy. Beat in the egg.

3 Sift the flour, cocoa powder, bicarbonate of soda and salt into the bowl and stir together. Add the buttermilk and stir until combined.

4 Using a level 5-cm/2-inch ice cream scoop or heaped tablespoon, put the mixture onto the prepared baking sheets in 5-cm/2-inch-diameter rounds about 3 cm/1¼ inches high and leaving at least 7.5 cm/3 inches between each round to allow room for spreading, or in the prepared pan.

5 Bake in the oven for 10–12 minutes, until firm to the touch. Transfer to a wire rack and leave to cool.

6 When the whoopies are cold, match each whoopie half with its closest partner in size. Spreading with a palette knife or using a piping bag fitted with a large star nozzle, cover the flat side of one whoopie half of each pair generously with the filling. Top each with its matching half, flat-side down, and press gently together.

Plus One: Ice Cool

Wrap each filled whoopie individually in clingfilm and freeze. To serve, allow to soften slightly at room temperature for about 30 minutes before eating like an ice cream sandwich. Alternatively, fill the whoopies with ice cream and serve immediately.

Red Velvet Whoopies

Makes 10

125 ml/4 fl oz buttermilk
½ tsp vanilla extract
½ tsp red paste food
    colouring
1½ tsp distilled white vinegar
115 g/4 oz butter, softened,
    plus extra for greasing
200 g/7 oz granulated sugar
1 large egg
280 g/10 oz white plain flour
1 tbsp cocoa powder
½ tsp bicarbonate of soda
pinch of salt

Filling
Cream Cheese Filling
    (see page 76)

An American delight, red velvet is a rich, dark red chocolate cake. It gets its colour from red food colouring, although grated beetroot was traditionally used. During the 1920s, it was a signature cake at the Waldorf-Astoria Hotel in New York and, according to legend, when a guest asked for the recipe, she was billed such an exorbitant amount that she spread the recipe via a chain letter.

1 Preheat the oven to 190°C/170°C fan/375°F/Gas Mark 5. Line 3–4 large baking sheets with baking paper or grease the wells of a whoopie pan.

2 Stir the buttermilk, vanilla extract, red food colouring and vinegar in a jug.

3 Put the butter and sugar in an electric mixer bowl, or use a large mixing bowl and a hand-held electric mixer, and whisk together until light and fluffy. Beat in the egg.

4 Sift the flour, cocoa powder, bicarbonate of soda and salt into the bowl and stir together. Add the buttermilk mixture and stir until combined.

5 Using a level 5-cm/2-inch ice cream scoop or heaped tablespoon, put the mixture onto the prepared baking sheets in 5-cm/2-inch-diameter rounds about 3 cm/1¼ inches high and leaving at least 7.5 cm/3 inches between each round to allow room for spreading, or in the prepared pan.

6 Bake in the oven for 10–12 minutes, until firm to the touch. Transfer to a wire rack and leave to cool.

7 When the whoopies are cold, match each whoopie half with its closest partner in size. Spreading with a palette knife or using a piping bag fitted with a large star nozzle, cover the flat side of one whoopie half of each pair generously with the filling. Top each with its matching half, flat-side down, and press gently together.

Plus One: Black & White Red Velvet

Sift 175 g/6 oz icing sugar into a bowl. Add 6 teaspoons hot water and stir until smooth and thick enough to coat the back of a wooden spoon. Transfer half the mixture to another bowl and mix in 3 tablespoons cocoa powder until smooth and thick enough to coat the back of the spoon. Coat each whoopie so that each half has a different icing. Leave to set.

Carrot Cake Whoopies

Makes 12

2 carrots, 225 g/8 oz total
    weight
50 g/1¾ oz walnuts or
    pecan nuts
115 g/4 oz butter, softened,
    plus extra for greasing
200 g/7 oz soft light brown
    sugar
1 tsp vanilla extract
1 large egg
350 g/12 oz white plain flour
1 tsp baking powder
1 tsp bicarbonate of soda
1 tsp ground cinnamon
½ tsp ground ginger
½ tsp grated nutmeg
pinch of salt
4 tbsp orange juice

Filling
Cream Cheese Filling
    (see page 76)

**Grated carrot adds sweetness to these whoopies, which are
sandwiched together with Cream Cheese Filling in a much loved
pairing. Serve them any time, but they are especially appropriate
for Easter, carrots being the Easter bunny's favourite food.**

1 Preheat the oven to 190°C/170°C fan/375°F/Gas Mark 5. Line 3–4 large baking sheets
   with baking paper or grease the wells of a whoopie pan.

2 Grate the carrots and finely chop the nuts.

3 Put the butter, sugar and vanilla extract in an electric mixer bowl, or use a large
   mixing bowl and a hand-held electric mixer, and whisk together until light and fluffy.
   Beat in the egg.

4 Sift the flour, baking powder, bicarbonate of soda, cinnamon, ginger, nutmeg
   and salt into the bowl and stir together until combined. Fold in the nuts, carrots
   and orange juice.

5 Using a level 5-cm/2-inch ice cream scoop or heaped tablespoon, put the mixture onto
   the prepared baking sheets in 5-cm/2-inch-diameter rounds about 3 cm/1¼ inches high
   and leaving at least 7.5 cm/3 inches between each round to allow room for spreading,
   or in the prepared pan.

6 Bake in the oven for 10–12 minutes, until firm to the touch. Transfer to a wire rack
   and leave to cool.

7 When the whoopies are cold, match each whoopie half with its closest partner in
   size. Spreading with a palette knife or using a piping bag fitted with a large star
   nozzle, cover the flat side of one whoopie half of each pair generously with the
   filling. Top each with its matching half, flat-side down, and press gently together.

Plus One: Carrot & Chocolate Chip

Instead of the walnuts or pecan nuts, use the same quantity of plain chocolate chips.

Gluten-free Chocolate Whoopies

Makes 12

115 g/4 oz butter, softened, plus extra for greasing
200 g/7 oz soft dark brown sugar
1 large egg
280 g/10 oz gluten-free white plain flour
50 g/1¾ oz cocoa powder
1½ tsp gluten-free baking powder
½ tsp bicarbonate of soda
pinch of salt
225 ml/8 fl oz buttermilk

Filling
Home-made Marshmallow Crème (see page 75) or Classic Marshmallow Filling (see page 73)

No one needs to feel left out when it comes to enjoying whoopies, even those who have an intolerance to gluten. So if you or a friend can't eat gluten, you can still safely tuck into these.

1 Preheat the oven to 190°C/170°C fan/375°F/Gas Mark 5. Line 3–4 large baking sheets with baking paper or grease the wells of a whoopie pan.

2 Put the butter and sugar in an electric mixer bowl, or use a large mixing bowl and a hand-held electric mixer, and whisk together until light and fluffy. Beat in the egg.

3 Sift the flour, cocoa powder, baking powder, bicarbonate of soda and salt into the bowl and stir together. Add the buttermilk and stir until combined.

4 Using a level 5-cm/2-inch ice cream scoop or heaped tablespoon, put the mixture onto the prepared baking sheets in 5-cm/2-inch-diameter rounds about 3 cm/1¼ inches high and leaving at least 7.5 cm/3 inches between each round to allow room for spreading, or in the prepared pan.

5 Bake in the oven for 10–12 minutes, until firm to the touch. Transfer to a wire rack and leave to cool.

6 When the whoopies are cold, match each whoopie half with its closest partner in size. Spreading with a palette knife or using a piping bag fitted with a large star nozzle, cover the flat side of one whoopie half of each pair generously with the filling. Top each with its matching half, flat-side down, and press gently together.

Plus One: Gluten-free Cinnamon & Yogurt

Omit the cocoa powder and increase the flour to 350 g/12 oz. Sift 1 teaspoon ground cinnamon in with the dry ingredients in Step 3 and use 225 g/8 oz natural yogurt in place of the buttermilk.

Peanut Butter Whoopies

Makes 12

55 g/2 oz butter, softened,
  plus extra for greasing
200 g/7 oz soft light brown
  sugar
75 g/2¾ oz smooth or crunchy
  peanut butter
1 tsp vanilla extract
1 large egg
350 g/12 oz white plain flour
1 tsp bicarbonate of soda
pinch of salt
225 ml/8 fl oz buttermilk

Filling

375 g/13 oz smooth or
  crunchy peanut butter and
  250 g/9 oz Marshmallow
  Fluff or Home-made
  Marshmallow Crème (see
  page 75) or Peanut Butter
  Filling (see page 76)

Peanut butter and Marshmallow Fluff is a classic combination in sandwiches and these whoopies are sure to appeal to peanut butter lovers everywhere.

1 Preheat the oven to 190°C/170°C fan/375°F/Gas Mark 5. Line 3–4 large baking sheets with baking paper or grease the wells of a whoopie pan.

2 Put the butter, sugar, peanut butter and vanilla extract in an electric mixer bowl, or use a large mixing bowl and a hand-held electric mixer, and whisk together until light and fluffy. Beat in the egg.

3 Sift the flour, bicarbonate of soda and salt into the bowl and stir together. Add the buttermilk and stir until combined.

4 Using a level 5-cm/2-inch ice cream scoop or heaped tablespoon, put the mixture onto the prepared baking sheets in 5-cm/2-inch-diameter rounds about 3 cm/1¼ inches high and leaving at least 7.5 cm/3 inches between each round to allow room for spreading, or in the prepared pan.

5 Bake in the oven for 10–12 minutes, until firm to the touch. Transfer to a wire rack and leave to cool.

6 When the whoopies are cold, match each whoopie half with its closest partner in size. Spreading with a palette knife, cover the flat side of one whoopie half of each pair with peanut butter, then with Marshmallow Fluff or Home-made Marshmallow Crème. Alternatively, spread generously with Peanut Butter Filling. Top each with its matching half, flat-side down, and press gently together.

Plus One: Peanut Butter & Banana

Break a small banana into a large bowl, add ¼ teaspoon lemon juice and mash with a fork. Sift in 600 g/1 lb 5 oz icing sugar. Add 55 g/2 oz softened butter and beat together until smooth. Use to fill the whoopies in place of the filling options above.

Summer

Reverse Classic Whoopies

Makes 12

115 g/4 oz butter, softened,
    plus extra for greasing
200 g/7 oz granulated sugar
1 tsp vanilla extract
1 large egg
350 g/12 oz white plain flour
1¼ tsp bicarbonate of soda
pinch of salt
225 ml/8 fl oz buttermilk
sifted icing sugar, for dusting

Filling
Chocolate Buttercream
    (see page 73)

This recipe turns the traditional formula of Classic Whoopies (see page 20), namely chocolate sponge with a cream filling, on its head to offer two vanilla-flavoured whoopies sandwiched together with a sumptuous chocolate filling.

1 Preheat the oven to 190°C/170°C fan/375°F/Gas Mark 5. Line 3–4 large baking sheets with baking paper or grease the wells of a whoopie pan.

2 Put the butter, sugar and vanilla extract in an electric mixer bowl, or use a large mixing bowl and a hand-held electric mixer, and whisk together until light and fluffy. Beat in the egg.

3 Sift the flour, bicarbonate of soda and salt into the bowl and stir together. Add the buttermilk and stir until combined.

4 Using a level 5-cm/2-inch ice cream scoop or heaped tablespoon, put the mixture onto the prepared baking sheets in 5-cm/2-inch-diameter rounds about 3 cm/1¼ inches high and leaving at least 7.5 cm/3 inches between each round to allow room for spreading, or in the prepared pan.

5 Bake in the oven for 10–12 minutes, until firm to the touch. Transfer to a wire rack and leave to cool.

6 When the whoopies are cold, match each whoopie half with its closest partner in size. Spreading with a palette knife or using a piping bag fitted with a large star nozzle, cover the flat side of one whoopie half of each pair generously with the filling. Top each with its matching half, flat-side down, and press gently together.

7 Serve dusted with sifted icing sugar.

Plus One: Vanilla & Cardamom

Split a vanilla pod lengthways with a sharp knife, scrape out the seeds and add to the cake mixture in place of the vanilla extract. Additionally, sift ¼ teaspoon ground cardamom in with the dry ingredients in Step 3, and, when making the buttercream, sift ½ teaspoon ground cardamom in with the icing sugar and cocoa powder.

Creamy Strawberry Whoopies

Makes 10

125 ml/4 fl oz buttermilk
½ tsp vanilla extract
1½ tsp distilled white vinegar
115 g/4 oz butter, softened,
 plus extra for greasing
200 g/7 oz granulated sugar
1 large egg
300 g/10½ oz white plain flour
½ tsp bicarbonate of soda
pinch of salt
pink sugar flowers,
 to decorate

Filling
115 g/4 oz full-fat cream
 cheese
55 g/2 oz butter, softened
450 g/1 lb icing sugar
4 tbsp seedless strawberry
 conserve

Topping
175 g/6 oz icing sugar
5–6 tsp hot water
red paste or liquid food
 colouring

While no one could describe a whoopie as 'dainty' as cakes go, these are undeniably and unashamedly pretty and 'girlie'.

1 Preheat the oven to 190°C/170°C fan/375°F/Gas Mark 5. Line 3–4 large baking sheets with baking paper or grease the wells of a whoopie pan.

2 Put the buttermilk, vanilla extract and vinegar in a jug and stir together.

3 Put the butter and sugar in an electric mixer bowl, or use a large mixing bowl and a hand-held electric mixer, and whisk together until light and fluffy. Beat in the egg.

4 Sift the flour, bicarbonate of soda and salt into the bowl and stir together. Add the buttermilk mixture and stir until combined.

5 Using a level 5-cm/2-inch ice cream scoop or heaped tablespoon, put the mixture onto the prepared baking sheets in 5-cm/2-inch-diameter rounds about 3 cm/1¼ inches high and leaving at least 7.5 cm/3 inches between each round to allow room for spreading, or in the prepared pan.

6 Bake in the oven for 10–12 minutes, until firm to the touch. Transfer to a wire rack and leave to cool.

7 To make the filling, put the cream cheese and butter in a large bowl and beat together until smooth. Sift in the icing sugar. Add the strawberry conserve and beat together until combined.

8 When the whoopies are cold, match each whoopie half with its closest partner in size. Spreading with a palette knife or using a piping bag fitted with a large star nozzle, cover the flat side of one whoopie half of each pair generously with the filling. Top each with its matching half, flat-side down, and press gently together.

9 To make the topping, sift the icing sugar into a bowl. Add the water and stir until the mixture is smooth and thick enough to coat the back of a wooden spoon. Dip the tip of a skewer into the food colouring, add to the icing and stir until evenly coloured. Spoon the icing on top of each filled whoopie. Decorate with sugar flowers and leave to set.

Plus One: Creamy Raspberry

Use seedless raspberry jam instead of the strawberry conserve in the filling.

Black Forest Whoopies

Makes 12

115 g/4 oz butter, softened,
    plus extra for greasing
200 g/7 oz granulated sugar
½ tsp vanilla extract
1 large egg
280 g/10 oz white plain flour
50 g/1¾ oz cocoa powder
2½ tsp baking powder
pinch of salt
225 ml/8 fl oz milk

Filling

425 g/15 oz canned stoned
    black cherries
2 tbsp kirsch
300 ml/½ pint double cream

Here, chocolate whoopies are luxuriously filled with black cherries and whipped cream, and moistened with a kirsch-laced syrup to make mini versions of the beloved Black Forest Gâteau. These are ideal served as a dessert – strictly for grown-ups, of course.

1 Preheat the oven to 190°C/170°C fan/375°F/Gas Mark 5. Line 3–4 large baking sheets with baking paper or grease the wells of a whoopie pan.

2 Put the butter, sugar and vanilla extract in an electric mixer bowl, or use a large mixing bowl and a hand-held electric mixer, and whisk together until light and fluffy. Beat in the egg.

3 Sift the flour, cocoa powder, baking powder and salt into the bowl and stir together. Add the milk and stir until combined.

4 Using a level 5-cm/2-inch ice cream scoop or heaped tablespoon, put the mixture onto the prepared baking sheets in 5-cm/2-inch-diameter rounds about 3 cm/1¼ inches high and leaving at least 7.5 cm/3 inches between each round to allow room for spreading, or in the prepared pan.

5 Bake in the oven for 10–12 minutes, until firm to the touch. Transfer to a wire rack and leave to cool.

6 To make the filling, drain the canned cherries, reserving the juice. Slice the cherries in half. Put 2 tablespoons of the reserved juice in a bowl and stir in the kirsch. In a separate large bowl, whip the cream until stiff.

7 When the whoopies are cold, match each whoopie half with its closest partner in size. Spreading with a palette knife or using a piping bag fitted with a large star nozzle, cover the flat side of the whoopie half of each pair generously with the whipped cream. Scatter the cherries on top. Top each with its matching half, flat-side down, and press gently together. Drizzle a teaspoon of the kirsch syrup over the top of each whoopie.

Plus One: Bursting Blueberry

Use 225 g/8 oz fresh whole blueberries instead of the cherries and omit the kirsch. Fill the whoopies with the whipped cream as above and scatter over the blueberries.

Apricot & Almond Whoopies

Makes 12

75 g/2¾ oz ready-to-eat dried
  apricots
55 g/2 oz butter, softened,
  plus extra for greasing
50 g/1¾ oz ground almonds
200 g/7 oz granulated sugar
½ tsp almond extract
1 large egg
350 g/12 oz white plain flour
1 tsp bicarbonate of soda
pinch of salt
225 ml/8 fl oz buttermilk

Filling
Almond Buttercream
  (see page 73)

Two convenient storecupboard ingredients – dried apricots and ground almonds – are the feature flavourings in this whoopie recipe, and they were simply made for each other.

1 Preheat the oven to 190°C/170°C fan/375°F/Gas Mark 5. Line 3–4 large baking sheets with baking paper or grease the wells of a whoopie pan.

2 Put the apricots in a food processor and pulse in short bursts until finely chopped.

3 Put the butter, ground almonds, sugar and almond extract in an electric mixer bowl, or use a large mixing bowl and a hand-held electric mixer, and whisk together until light and fluffy. Beat in the egg.

4 Sift the flour, bicarbonate of soda and salt into the bowl and stir together. Add the buttermilk and chopped apricots and stir until combined.

5 Using a level 5-cm/2-inch ice cream scoop or heaped tablespoon, put the mixture onto the prepared baking sheets in 5-cm/2-inch-diameter rounds about 3 cm/1¼ inches high and leaving at least 7.5 cm/3 inches between each round to allow room for spreading, or in the prepared pan.

6 Bake in the oven for 10–12 minutes, until firm to the touch. Transfer to a wire rack and leave to cool.

7 When the whoopies are cold, match each whoopie half with its closest partner in size. Spreading with a palette knife or using a piping bag fitted with a large star nozzle, cover the flat side of one whoopie half of each pair generously with the filling. Top each with its matching half, flat-side down, and press gently together.

Plus One: Cherry & Almond

Replace the apricots with the same quantity of glacé cherries, chopping them by hand instead of in a food processor.

Bashed Banana Whoopies

Makes 10

2 bananas
1 tsp lemon juice
115 g/4 oz butter, softened,
    plus extra for greasing
200 g/7 oz soft light brown
    sugar
1 tsp vanilla extract
1 large egg
280 g/10 oz white plain flour
½ tsp ground cinnamon
1 tsp baking powder
1 tsp bicarbonate of soda
pinch of salt
3 tbsp soured cream

Filling
125 g/4½ oz butter, softened
300 g/10½ oz icing sugar
1 tbsp milk
1 tbsp honey

Packed with good-for-you bananas, perhaps these moist whoopies could almost be classed as health food! Whatever else, they are sure to enhance well-being by lifting the spirits.

1 Preheat the oven to 190°C/170°C fan/375°F/Gas Mark 5. Line 3–4 large baking sheets with baking paper or grease the wells of a whoopie pan.

2 Break the bananas into a bowl. Add the lemon juice and mash together with a fork until smooth.

3 Put the butter, sugar and vanilla extract in an electric mixer bowl, or use a large mixing bowl and a hand-held electric mixer, and whisk together until light and fluffy. Beat in the egg.

4 Sift the flour, cinnamon, baking powder, bicarbonate of soda and salt into the bowl and stir together. Add the mashed bananas and soured cream and stir until combined.

5 Using a level 5-cm/2-inch ice cream scoop or heaped tablespoon, put the mixture onto the prepared baking sheets in 5-cm/2-inch-diameter rounds about 3 cm/1¼ inches high and leaving at least 7.5 cm/3 inches between each round to allow room for spreading, or in the prepared pan.

6 Bake in the oven for 10 minutes, until firm to the touch. Transfer to a wire rack and leave to cool.

7 To make the filling, put the butter in a large bowl. Sift in the icing sugar. Add the milk and honey and beat together until smooth.

8 When the whoopies are cold, match each whoopie half with its closest partner in size. Spreading with a palette knife or using a piping bag fitted with a large star nozzle, cover the flat side of one whoopie half of each pair generously with the filling. Top each with its matching half, flat-side down, and press gently together.

Plus One: Banana & Passion Fruit

Cut 4 passion fruits in half, scoop out the pulp and put in a small saucepan. Add 4 tablespoons honey and heat gently until warmed through. Spoon the mixture over the filled whoopies.

Autumn

Pumpkin Whoopies

Makes 12

115 g/4 oz butter, softened,
    plus extra for greasing
200 g/7 oz soft light brown
    sugar
1 tsp vanilla extract
1 large egg
350 g/12 oz white plain flour
1 tsp baking powder
1 tsp bicarbonate of soda
1 tsp ground cinnamon
½ tsp ground ginger
¼ tsp ground allspice or
    grated nutmeg
¼ tsp ground cloves
pinch of salt
225 g/8 oz canned or fresh
    pumpkin purée
2 tbsp buttermilk

Filling
Cream Cheese Filling
    (see page 76)

Although sure to be popular all the year round, these sweet-spicy pumpkin-packed whoopies are particularly good for Halloween or Thanksgiving. You could even serve them as a contemporary take on the traditional pumpkin pie.

1 Preheat the oven to 190°C/170°C fan/375°F/Gas Mark 5. Line 3–4 large baking sheets with baking paper or grease the wells of a whoopie pan.

2 Put the butter, sugar and vanilla extract in an electric mixer bowl, or use a large mixing bowl and a hand-held electric mixer, and whisk together until light and fluffy. Beat in the egg.

3 Sift the flour, baking powder, bicarbonate of soda, cinnamon, ginger, allspice, cloves and salt into the bowl and stir together. Add the pumpkin purée and buttermilk and stir until combined.

4 Using a level 5-cm/2-inch ice cream scoop or heaped tablespoon, put the mixture onto the prepared baking sheets in 5-cm/2-inch-diameter rounds about 3 cm/1¼ inches high and leaving at least 7.5 cm/3 inches between each round to allow room for spreading, or in the prepared pan.

5 Bake in the oven for 10–12 minutes, until firm to the touch. Transfer to a wire rack and leave to cool.

6 When the whoopies are cold, match each whoopie half with its closest partner in size. Spreading with a palette knife or using a piping bag fitted with a large star nozzle, cover the flat side of one whoopie half of each pair generously with the filling. Top each with its matching half, flat-side down, and press gently together.

Plus One: Pumpkin & Banana

Slice 2 bananas, put in a bowl and toss with ½ teaspoon lemon juice. Spread half the quantity of Cream Cheese Filling called for above on one half of each pair of whoopies, arrange the sliced bananas on top and cover each with its matching half.

Chocolate Chunk & Oat Whoopies

Makes 12

115 g/4 oz butter, softened,
   plus extra for greasing
200 g/7 oz soft light brown
   sugar
½ tsp vanilla extract
1 large egg
300 g/10½ oz white plain flour
2½ tsp baking powder
pinch of salt
100 g/3½ oz plain chocolate
   chunks
50 g/1¾ oz porridge oats
4 tbsp buttermilk

Filling
Vanilla Buttercream
   (see page 73)

Plain chocolate chunks are always irresistible. But combined with oats for extra crunch, they make these whoopies especially satisfying – as well as dangerously moreish.

1 Preheat the oven to 190°C/170°C fan/375°F/Gas Mark 5. Line 3–4 large baking sheets with baking paper or butter the wells of a whoopie pan.

2 Put the butter, sugar and vanilla extract in an electric mixer bowl, or use a large mixing bowl and a hand-held electric mixer, and whisk together until light and fluffy. Beat in the egg.

3 Sift the flour, baking powder and salt into the bowl and stir together. Add the chocolate chunks, oats and buttermilk and stir until combined.

4 Using a level 5-cm/2-inch ice cream scoop or heaped tablespoon, put the mixture onto the prepared baking sheets in 5-cm/2-inch-diameter rounds about 3 cm/1¼ inches high and leaving at least 7.5 cm/3 inches between each round to allow room for spreading, or in the prepared pan.

5 Bake in the oven for 10–12 minutes, until firm to the touch. Transfer to a wire rack and leave to cool.

6 When the whoopies are cold, match each whoopie half with its closest partner in size. Spreading with a palette knife or using a piping bag fitted with a large star nozzle, cover the flat side of one whoopie half of each pair generously with the filling. Top each with its matching half, flat-side down, and press gently together.

Plus One: Soft Fudge

In place of the chocolate chunks, add the same quantity of fudge pieces to the whoopie cake mixture, and replace the filling with Butterscotch Filling (see page 78).

Moist Apple & Almond Whoopies

Makes 10

2 apples
½ tsp lemon juice
115 g/4 oz butter, softened,
    plus extra for greasing
200 g/7 oz granulated sugar
½ tsp almond extract
1 large egg
350 g/12 oz white plain flour
2½ tsp baking powder
pinch of salt
10 g/¼ oz flaked almonds

Filling
Vanilla Buttercream
    (see page 73)

This is another winning fruit 'n' nut combination. Grated apples bring a pleasing moistness to the whoopies, while almond extract enhances their flavour without the addition of relatively expensive ground almonds – although you would never guess.

1 Preheat the oven to 190°C/170°C fan/375°F/Gas Mark 5. Line 3–4 large baking sheets with baking paper or grease the wells of a whoopie pan.

2 Peel, core and grate the apples. Put in a bowl, add the lemon juice and toss together.

3 Put the butter, sugar and almond extract in an electric mixer bowl, or use a large mixing bowl and a hand-held electric mixer, and whisk together until light and fluffy. Beat in the egg.

4 Sift the flour, baking powder and salt into the bowl and stir together. Add the grated apple and stir until combined.

5 Using a level 5-cm/2-inch ice cream scoop or heaped tablespoon, put the mixture onto the prepared baking sheets in 5-cm/2-inch-diameter rounds about 3 cm/1¼ inches high and leaving at least 7.5 cm/3 inches between each round to allow room for spreading, or in the prepared pan.

6 Sprinkle the flaked almonds equally on top of 10 of the mounds of mixture.

7 Bake in the oven for 10–12 minutes, until firm to the touch. Transfer to a wire rack and leave to cool.

8 When the whoopies are cold, match each almond-topped whoopie half with its closest partner in size. Spreading with a palette knife or using a piping bag fitted with a large star nozzle, cover the flat side of each whoopie half without almonds generously with the filling. Top each with its matching almond-topped half, flat-side down, and press gently together.

Plus One: Toffee Apple

Omit the almond extract and flaked almonds. Fill the whoopies with Caramel Buttercream (see page 73) and drizzle 1 teaspoon dulce de leche over the top of each.

Green Pistachio Whoopies

Makes 10

60 g/2¼ oz shelled pistachio
   nuts
125 ml/4 fl oz buttermilk
½ tsp vanilla extract
½ tsp green paste food
   colouring
1½ tsp distilled white vinegar
115 g/4 oz butter, softened,
   plus extra for greasing
200 g/7 oz granulated sugar
1 large egg
280 g/10 oz white plain flour
½ tsp bicarbonate of soda
pinch of salt

Filling
**Home-made Marshmallow
   Crème (see page 75)
   or Classic Marshmallow
   Filling (see page 73)**

There's no other way to describe these – whoopies tinted an attractive shade of green to reflect the distinctive colour of the finely chopped pistachio nuts that flavour them.

1 Preheat the oven to 190°C/170°C fan/375°F/Gas Mark 5. Line 3–4 large baking sheets with baking paper or grease the wells of a whoopie pan.

2 Finely chop the pistachio nuts.

3 Put the buttermilk, vanilla extract, green food colouring and vinegar in a jug and stir together.

4 Put the butter and sugar in an electric mixer bowl, or use a large mixing bowl and a hand-held electric mixer, and whisk together until light and fluffy. Beat in the egg.

5 Sift the flour, bicarbonate of soda and salt into the bowl and stir together. Add the chopped pistachio nuts, reserving 1 tablespoon, and the buttermilk mixture and beat until well combined.

6 Using a level 5-cm/2-inch ice cream scoop or heaped tablespoon, put the mixture onto the prepared baking sheets in 5-cm/2-inch-diameter rounds about 3 cm/1¼ inches high and leaving at least 7.5 cm/3 inches between each round to allow room for spreading, or in the prepared pan. Sprinkle the reserved pistachio nuts equally on top of 10 of the mounds of mixture.

7 Bake in the oven for 10–12 minutes, until firm to the touch. Transfer to a wire rack and leave to cool.

8 When the whoopies are cold, match each pistachio-topped whoopie half with its closest partner in size. Spreading with a palette knife or using a piping bag fitted with a large star nozzle, cover the flat side of each whoopie half without pistachios generously with the filling. Top each with its matching pistachio-topped half, flat-side down, and press gently together.

Plus One: Crunchy Hazelnut

Omit the food colouring and replace the pistachio nuts with hazelnuts, both in the mixture and for sprinkling. Instead of the filling, spread the whoopie halves without hazelnuts generously with shop-bought hazelnut-and-chocolate spread, then sprinkle with 115 g/4 oz chopped hazelnuts before covering with the matching hazelnut-topped halves.

Mocha Whoopies

Makes 9

3 tbsp instant espresso
    coffee
1 tbsp boiling water
115 g/4 oz butter, softened,
    plus extra for greasing
200 g/7 oz soft dark brown
    sugar
1 large egg
280 g/10 oz white plain flour
50 g/1¾ oz cocoa powder
1¼ tsp bicarbonate of soda
pinch of salt
2 tbsp buttermilk

Filling
Chocolate Marshmallow
    Crème (see page 75)

Dark, rich and seductive, these modish mini mochas are guaranteed to appeal to coffee and chocolate addicts alike.

1 Preheat the oven to 190°C/170°C fan/375°F/Gas Mark 5. Line 3–4 large baking sheets with baking paper or grease the wells of a whoopie pan.

2 Dissolve the coffee in the boiling water and set aside to cool.

3 Put the butter and sugar in an electric mixer bowl, or use a large mixing bowl and a hand-held electric mixer, and whisk together until light and fluffy. Beat in the egg.

4 Sift the flour, cocoa powder, bicarbonate of soda and salt into the bowl and stir together. Add the coffee and buttermilk and stir until combined.

5 Using a level 5-cm/2-inch ice cream scoop or heaped tablespoon, put the mixture onto the prepared baking sheets in 5-cm/2-inch-diameter rounds about 3 cm/1¼ inches high and leaving at least 7.5 cm/3 inches between each round to allow room for spreading, or in the prepared pan.

6 Bake in the oven for 10–12 minutes, until firm to the touch. Transfer to a wire rack and leave to cool.

7 When the whoopies are cold, match each whoopie half with its closest partner in size. Spreading with a palette knife or using a piping bag fitted with a large star nozzle, cover the flat side of one whoopie half of each pair generously with the filling. Top each with its matching half, flat-side down, and press gently together.

Plus One: Tiramisù

In place of the Chocolate Marshmallow Crème filling, put 115 g/4 oz mascarpone cheese and 70 g/2½ oz softened butter in a large bowl and beat together. Sift in 450 g/1 lb icing sugar and beat until combined. Use to fill the whoopies. Drizzle about 1 teaspoon Marsala over the top of each to finish.

Winter

Mint Chocolate Whoopies

Makes 12

115 g/4 oz butter, softened,
   plus extra for greasing
200 g/7 oz granulated sugar
1 tsp vanilla extract
1 large egg
280 g/10 oz white plain flour
50 g/1¾ oz cocoa powder
2½ tsp baking powder
pinch of salt
225 ml/8 fl oz milk
100 g/3½ oz plain chocolate
   chips

Filling
175 g/6 oz butter, softened
½ tsp mint extract
350 g/12 oz icing sugar
1 tbsp milk or cream
green paste or liquid food
   colouring

It's all in the filling – a cool green minty buttercream, contrasted against the warm brown of chocolate whoopies studded with chunky chocolate chips. In short, the perfect partnership.

1 Preheat the oven to 190°C/170°C fan/375°F/Gas Mark 5. Line 3–4 large baking sheets with baking paper or grease the wells of a whoopie pan.

2 Put the butter, sugar and vanilla extract in an electric mixer bowl, or use a large mixing bowl and a hand-held electric mixer, and whisk together until light and fluffy. Beat in the egg.

3 Sift the flour, cocoa powder, baking powder and salt into the bowl and stir together. Add the milk and chocolate chips and stir until combined.

4 Using a level 5-cm/2-inch ice cream scoop or heaped tablespoon, put the mixture onto the prepared baking sheets in 5-cm/2-inch-diameter rounds about 3 cm/1¼ inches high and leaving at least 7.5 cm/3 inches between each round to allow room for spreading, or in the prepared pan.

5 Bake in the oven for 10–12 minutes, until firm to the touch. Transfer to a wire rack and leave to cool.

6 For the filling, put the butter and mint extract in a large bowl and beat together with a wooden spoon until light and fluffy. Sift in the icing sugar. Add the milk and beat together until well blended. Dip the tip of a skewer into the food colouring, add to the filling and stir until evenly coloured to the shade that you want.

7 When the whoopies are cold, match each whoopie half with its closest partner in size. Spreading with a palette knife or using a piping bag fitted with a large star nozzle, cover the flat side of one whoopie half of each pair generously with the filling. Top each with its matching half, flat-side down, and press gently together.

Plus One: Chocolate & Ginger

Replace the mint filling with Ginger Buttercream (see page 73).

Gingerbread Whoopies

Makes 9

150 g/5½ oz butter, softened,
  plus extra for greasing
150 g/5½ oz soft dark brown
  sugar
1 tsp vanilla extract
1 large egg
2 tbsp molasses or black
  treacle
350 g/12 oz white plain flour
2½ tsp baking powder
1½ tsp ground ginger
¾ tsp ground mixed spice
pinch of salt
1 tbsp milk

Filling
Lemon Buttercream
  (see page 73)

This classic recipe is beloved by both children and adults. The whoopies are filled with a zesty lemon-flavoured buttercream, which provides the ideal foil for the warm, mellow spices.

1 Preheat the oven to 190°C/170°C fan/375°F/Gas Mark 5. Line 3–4 large baking sheets with baking paper or grease the wells of a whoopie pan.

2 Put the butter, sugar and vanilla extract in an electric mixer bowl, or use a large mixing bowl and a hand-held electric mixer, and whisk together until light and fluffy. Add the egg and molasses and beat together.

3 Sift the flour, baking powder, ginger, mixed spice and salt into the bowl and stir together. Add the milk and stir until combined.

4 Using a level 5-cm/2-inch ice cream scoop or heaped tablespoon, put the mixture onto the prepared baking sheets in 5-cm/2-inch-diameter rounds about 3 cm/1¼ inches high and leaving at least 7.5 cm/3 inches between each round to allow room for spreading, or in the prepared pan.

5 Bake in the oven for 10–12 minutes, until firm to the touch. Transfer to a wire rack and leave to cool.

6 When the whoopies are cold, match each whoopie half with its closest partner in size. Spreading with a palette knife or using a piping bag fitted with a large star nozzle, cover the flat side of one whoopie half of each pair generously with the filling. Top each with its matching half, flat-side down, and press gently together.

Plus One: Brown Sugar & Spice

For the whoopie mixture, omit the ground ginger and increase the mixed spice to 2 teaspoons. Instead of the buttercream, fill the whoopies with Butterscotch Filling (see page 78).

Citrus Orange Whoopies

Makes 10

150 g/5½ oz butter, softened,
    plus extra for greasing
150 g/5½ oz granulated sugar
1 large egg
350 g/12 oz white plain flour
2½ tsp baking powder
pinch of salt
finely grated rind of
    2 oranges
3 tbsp orange juice
shredded orange rind,
    to decorate

Filling
Orange Buttercream
    (see page 73)

Topping
175 g/6 oz icing sugar
5–6 tsp orange juice
orange paste or liquid
    food colouring

These extra-soft whoopies offer bold orange flavour throughout – in the cake, filling, topping and even the final decorative touch.

1 Preheat the oven to 190°C/170°C fan/375°F/Gas Mark 5. Line 3–4 large baking sheets with baking paper or grease the wells of a whoopie pan.

2 Put the butter and sugar in an electric mixer bowl, or use a large mixing bowl and a hand-held electric mixer, and whisk together until light and fluffy. Beat in the egg.

3 Sift the flour, baking powder and salt into the bowl and stir together. Add the grated orange rind and juice and stir until combined.

4 Using a level 5-cm/2-inch ice cream scoop or heaped tablespoon, put the mixture onto the prepared baking sheets in 5-cm/2-inch-diameter rounds about 3 cm/1¼ inches high and leaving at least 7.5 cm/3 inches between each round to allow room for spreading, or in the prepared pan.

5 Bake in the oven for 10–12 minutes, until firm to the touch. Transfer to a wire rack and leave to cool.

6 When the whoopies are cold, match each whoopie half with its closest partner in size. Spreading with a palette knife or using a piping bag fitted with a large star nozzle, cover the flat side of one whoopie half of each pair generously with the filling. Top each with its matching half, flat-side down, and press gently together.

7 For the topping, sift the icing sugar into a bowl. Add the orange juice and stir until the mixture is smooth and thick enough to coat the back of a wooden spoon. Dip the tip of a skewer into the food colouring, add to the icing and stir until evenly coloured to the shade that you want.

8 Spoon the topping over each whoopie. Top with shredded orange rind to decorate and leave to set.

Plus One: Lemon & Poppy Seed

Replace the grated orange rind and juice with grated lemon rind and juice and add to the whoopie mixture along with 2 tablespoons poppy seeds. Instead of the buttercream, fill the whoopies with Cream Cheese Filling (see page 76) and decorate with shredded lemon-rind.

Very Chocolate Whoopies

Makes 12

100 g/3½ oz plain chocolate
   (minimum 70% cocoa
   solids)
115 g/4 oz butter, softened,
   plus extra for greasing
200 g/7 oz granulated sugar
1 tsp vanilla extract
1 large egg
280 g/10 oz white plain flour
50 g/1¾ oz cocoa powder
2½ tsp baking powder
pinch of salt
225 ml/8 fl oz milk
12 mini Oreo biscuits,
   to decorate

Filling
Oreo Cream Filling
   (see page 78)

Topping
Chocolate Ganache
   (see page 81)

Whoopie purists fervently believe that the whoopie should be chocolate and nothing else, while others view whoopies as the next best thing to Oreo biscuits. Combine the two and you get the very best chocolate whoopies ever. These are definitely ones for sharing.

1 Preheat the oven to 190°C/170°C fan/375°F/Gas Mark 5. Line 3–4 large baking sheets with baking paper or grease the wells of a whoopie pan.

2 Finely grate the chocolate or put in a food processor and process until very finely ground. Set aside.

3 Put the butter, sugar and vanilla extract in an electric mixer bowl, or use a large mixing bowl and a hand-held electric mixer, and whisk together until light and fluffy. Beat in the egg.

4 Sift the flour, cocoa powder, baking powder and salt into the bowl and stir together. Add the chocolate and milk and stir until combined.

5 Using a level 5-cm/2-inch ice cream scoop or heaped tablespoon, put the mixture onto the prepared baking sheets in 5-cm/2-inch-diameter rounds about 3 cm/1¼ inches high and leaving at least 7.5 cm/3 inches between each round to allow room for spreading, or in the prepared pan.

6 Bake in the oven for 10–12 minutes, until firm to the touch. Transfer to a wire rack and leave to cool.

7 When the whoopies are cold, match each whoopie half with its closest partner in size. Spreading with a palette knife or using a piping bag fitted with a large star nozzle, cover the flat side of one whoopie half of each pair generously with the filling.

8 Spread the Chocolate Ganache on top of the other whoopie halves, then place each on top of its matching bottom half and press gently together. Decorate each with a mini Oreo biscuit and leave to set.

Plus One: Chocolate & Butterscotch

Instead of the Oreo Cream Filling, use the Butterscotch Filling (see page 78) to fill the whoopies, omit the ganache topping and dust with sifted icing sugar before serving.

Pecan & Maple Syrup Whoopies

These whoopies are wonderfully moist and syrupy, and the addition of chopped pecan nuts gives them a little winter flair.

Makes 12

60 g/2¼ oz pecan halves
150 g/5½ oz butter, softened,
    plus extra for greasing
150 g/5½ oz soft light
    brown sugar
1 tsp vanilla extract
1 large egg
350 g/12 oz white plain flour
2½ tsp baking powder
pinch of salt
6 tbsp maple syrup
4 tbsp milk

Filling
Butterscotch Filling
    (see page 78)

1 Preheat the oven to 190°C/170°C fan/375°F/Gas Mark 5. Line 3–4 large baking sheets with baking paper or butter the wells of a whoopie pan.

2 Reserve 12 of the smallest pecan halves. Finely chop the remaining pecan halves and set aside.

3 Put the butter, sugar and vanilla extract in an electric mixer bowl, or use a large mixing bowl and a hand-held electric mixer, and whisk together until light and fluffy. Beat in the egg.

4 Sift the flour, baking powder and salt into the bowl and stir together. Add the chopped pecan nuts, maple syrup and milk and stir until combined.

5 Using a level 5-cm/2-inch ice cream scoop or heaped tablespoon, put the mixture onto the prepared baking sheets in 5-cm/2-inch-diameter rounds about 3 cm/1¼ inches high and leaving at least 7.5 cm/3 inches between each round to allow room for spreading, or in the prepared pan. Put one of the reserved pecan halves on top of each of 12 mounds of mixture.

6 Bake in the oven for 10–12 minutes, until firm to the touch. Transfer to a wire rack and leave to cool.

7 When the whoopies are cold, match each pecan-topped whoopie half with its closest partner in size. Spreading with a palette knife or using a piping bag fitted with a large star nozzle, cover the flat side of each whoopie half without a pecan generously with the filling. Top each with its matching half, flat-side down, and press gently together.

Plus One: Winter Walnut

Simply replace the pecan nuts with walnuts and use honey instead of the maple syrup.

Making Whoopies

Mix & Match

Having mastered the main whoopie recipes, this is the opportunity to get creative. The basic Chocolate Whoopies and the basic Vanilla Whoopies are the recipes that you will keep returning to. These are given here, along with a collection of all the fillings and toppings that you will ever need for easy reference. The possibilities are endless.

Vanilla Whoopies

Makes 12

115 g/4 oz butter, softened, plus extra for greasing
200 g/7 oz granulated sugar
1 tsp vanilla extract
1 large egg
350 g/12 oz white plain flour
1¼ tsp bicarbonate of soda
pinch of salt
225 ml/8 fl oz buttermilk

1 Preheat the oven to 190°C/170°C fan/375°F/Gas Mark 5. Line 3–4 large baking sheets with baking paper or grease the wells of a whoopie pan.

2 Put the butter, sugar and vanilla extract in an electric mixer bowl, or use a large mixing bowl and a hand-held electric mixer, and whisk together until light and fluffy. Beat in the egg.

3 Sift the flour, bicarbonate of soda and salt into the bowl and stir together. Add the buttermilk and stir until combined.

4 Using a level 5-cm/2-inch ice cream scoop or heaped tablespoon, put the mixture onto the prepared baking sheets in 5-cm/2-inch-diameter rounds about 3 cm/1¼ inches high and leaving at least 7.5 cm/3 inches between each round to allow room for spreading, or in the prepared pan.

5 Bake in the oven for 10–12 minutes, until firm to the touch. Transfer to a wire rack and leave to cool.

6 When the whoopies are cold, match each whoopie half with its closest partner in size and then fill and decorate as you wish.

Chocolate Whoopies

Makes 12
115 g/4 oz butter, softened, plus extra for greasing
200 g/7 oz soft dark brown sugar
1 tsp vanilla extract
1 large egg
280 g/10 oz white plain flour
50 g/1¾ oz cocoa powder
1¼ tsp bicarbonate of soda
pinch of salt
225 ml/8 fl oz buttermilk

1 Preheat the oven to 190°C/170°C fan/375°F/Gas Mark 5. Line 3–4 large baking sheets with baking paper or grease the wells of a whoopie pan.

2 Put the butter, sugar and vanilla extract in an electric mixer bowl, or use a large mixing bowl and a hand-held electric mixer, and whisk together until light and fluffy. Beat in the egg.

3 Sift the flour, cocoa powder, bicarbonate of soda and salt into the bowl and stir together. Add the buttermilk and stir until combined.

4 Using a level 5-cm/2-inch ice cream scoop or heaped tablespoon, put the mixture onto the prepared baking sheets in 5 cm/2 inch-diameter rounds about 3 cm/1¼ inches high and leaving at least 7.5 cm/3 inches between each round to allow room for spreading, or in the prepared pan.

5 Bake in the oven for 10–12 minutes, until firm to the touch. Transfer to a wire rack and leave to cool.

6 When the whoopies are cold, match each whoopie half with its closest partner in size and then fill and decorate as you wish.

Mini Chocolate Whoopies

Makes 24
115 g/4 oz butter, softened, plus extra for greasing
200 g/7 oz granulated sugar
½ tsp vanilla extract
1 large egg
280 g/10 oz white plain flour
50 g/1¾ oz cocoa powder
2½ tsp baking powder
pinch of salt
225 ml/8 fl oz milk

1 Preheat the oven to 190°C/170°C fan/375°F/Gas Mark 5. Line 3–4 large baking sheets with baking paper or grease the holes of a 24-hole mini muffin tin.

2 Put the butter, sugar and vanilla extract in an electric mixer bowl, or use a large mixing bowl and a hand-held electric mixer, and whisk together until light and fluffy. Beat in the egg.

3 Sift the flour, cocoa powder, baking powder and salt into the bowl and stir together. Add the milk and stir until combined.

4 Using a heaped teaspoon, put the mixture onto the prepared baking sheets, allowing room for spreading, or in the prepared tin.

5 Bake in the oven for 8–10 minutes, until firm to the touch. Transfer to a wire rack and leave to cool.

6 When cold, fill and decorate as you wish.

Mini Vanilla Whoopies

Makes 24
115 g/4 oz butter, softened, plus extra for greasing
200 g/7 oz granulated sugar
½ tsp vanilla extract
1 large egg
325 g/11½ oz white plain flour
2½ tsp baking powder
pinch of salt
225 ml/8 fl oz milk

1 Preheat the oven to 190°C/170°C fan/375°F/Gas Mark 5. Line 3–4 large baking sheets with baking paper or grease the holes of a 24-hole mini muffin tin.

2 Put the butter, sugar and vanilla extract in an electric mixer bowl, or use a large mixing bowl and a hand-held electric mixer, and whisk together until light and fluffy. Beat in the egg.

3 Sift the flour, baking powder and salt into the bowl and stir together. Add the milk and stir until combined.

4 Using a heaped teaspoon, put the mixture onto the prepared baking sheets, allowing room for spreading, or in the prepared tin.

5 Bake in the oven for 8–10 minutes, until firm to the touch. Transfer to a wire rack and leave to cool.

6 When cold, fill and decorate as you wish.

Vanilla Buttercream

Makes enough to fill 12 whoopies
175 g/6 oz butter, softened
¾ tsp vanilla extract
350 g/12 oz icing sugar
1 tbsp milk or cream

1 Put the butter and vanilla extract in a large bowl and beat together with a wooden spoon until combined.

2 Sift in the icing sugar. Add the milk and beat together until light and fluffy. Use immediately or store in the refrigerator for up to 1 week.

VARIATIONS

Chocolate Buttercream
Replace 50 g/1¾ oz of the icing sugar with the same quantity of cocoa powder.

Almond Buttercream
Replace the vanilla extract with ¾ tsp almond extract.

Coffee Buttercream
Dissolve 1 tablespoon instant espresso powder in 1 teaspoon boiling water. Leave until cold and use instead of the vanilla extract.

Caramel Buttercream
Add 2 tablespoons of dulce de leche with the milk.

Ginger Buttercream
Use the syrup from a jar of stem ginger in syrup instead of the milk or cream and add 4 pieces of finely chopped stem ginger to the buttercream.

Coloured Buttercream
Using paste or liquid food colouring of your choice, such as red, green or yellow, dip the tip of a skewer into the colouring, add to the buttercream and stir until evenly coloured to the shade that you want.

Orange or Lemon Buttercream
Replace the milk or cream with orange or lemon juice. Add a little finely grated rind, and colour with orange or yellow food colouring, as in Coloured Buttercream, if you wish.

Classic Marshmallow Filling

Makes enough to fill 12 whoopies
100 g/3½ oz icing sugar
115 g/4 oz butter or American vegetable shortening, softened
100 g/3½ oz Marshmallow Fluff
1 tsp vanilla extract

1 Sift the icing sugar into a bowl.

2 Put the butter and Marshmallow Fluff in an electric mixer bowl, or use a large mixing bowl and a hand-held electric mixer, and whisk together for about 3 minutes until light and fluffy.

3 On a low speed, gradually add the icing sugar in spoonfuls. Add the vanilla extract and beat together for about a further 3 minutes until combined.

4 Use immediately or store in the refrigerator for up to 2–3 days.

Home-made Marshmallow Crème

Makes enough to fill 12 whoopies
70 g/2½ oz icing sugar
1 large egg white
225 g/8 oz light corn or golden syrup
pinch of salt

1 Sift the icing sugar into a bowl.

2 Put the egg white, syrup and salt in an electric mixer bowl, or use a large mixing bowl and a hand-held electric mixer, and whisk on a high speed for 5 minutes until thick and doubled in volume.

3 On a low speed, gradually add the icing sugar in spoonfuls. Whisk until combined.

4 Use immediately or store in the refrigerator for up to 2–3 days. The filling suitable for spreading instead of piping into whoopies.

Chocolate Marshmallow Crème

Makes enough to fill 12 whoopies
50 g/1¾ oz plain chocolate
175 g/6 oz icing sugar
1 large egg white
115 g/4 oz light corn or golden syrup
pinch of salt

1 Break the chocolate into a heatproof bowl. Melt in a microwave oven on High for 30 seconds. Stir with a tablespoon. Cook again on High, checking and stirring every 10 seconds, until smooth. Alternatively, put the bowl over a saucepan of simmering water, making sure the bottom of the bowl doesn't touch the water, and stir until smooth. Leave until cold but not set.

2 Sift the icing sugar into a bowl.

3 Put the egg white, syrup and salt in an electric mixer bowl, or use a large mixing bowl and a hand-held electric mixer, and whisk on a high speed for 5 minutes until thick and doubled in volume.

4 On a low speed, gradually add the icing sugar in spoonfuls. Add the melted chocolate and whisk until just combined.

5 Chill in the refrigerator for 3–4 hours before using and store for up to 2–3 days. The filling suitable for spreading instead of piping into whoopies.

Peanut Butter Filling

Makes enough to fill 12 whoopies
275 g/9¾ oz smooth or crunchy peanut butter
140 g/5 oz butter, softened
115 g/4 oz icing sugar

1 Put the peanut butter and butter in a large bowl and beat together with a wooden spoon until smooth.

2 Sift in the icing sugar and beat together until light and fluffy. Use immediately or store in the refrigerator for up to 2–3 days.

Cream Cheese Filling

Makes enough to fill 12 whoopies
115 g/4 oz full-fat cream cheese
70 g/2½ oz butter, softened
½ tsp vanilla extract
450 g/1 lb icing sugar

1 Put the cream cheese, butter and vanilla extract in a large bowl and beat together with a wooden spoon until light and fluffy.

2 Sift in the icing sugar and beat together until well combined. Use immediately or store in the refrigerator for up to 2–3 days.

Butterscotch Filling

Makes enough to fill 12 whoopies
55 g/2 oz butter
100 g/3½ oz soft light brown sugar
90 ml/3 fl oz evaporated milk
400 g/14 oz icing sugar
½ tsp vanilla extract

1 Put the butter, sugar and evaporated milk in a saucepan. Heat gently, stirring all the time, until the butter has melted. Remove from the heat and leave to cool slightly.

2 Sift in the icing sugar. Add the vanilla extract and beat well until combined. Leave to cool before using. Store in the refrigerator for up to 1 week.

Oreo Cream Filling

Makes enough to fill 12 whoopies
3 Oreo cookies
55 g/2 oz butter, softened
115 g/4 oz full-fat cream cheese
350 g/12 oz icing sugar

1 Put the biscuits in a strong polythene bag and, holding the open end together, crush with a rolling pin to form fine crumbs.

2 Put the butter and cream cheese in an electric mixer bowl, or use a large mixing bowl and a hand-held electric mixer, and whisk together until light and fluffy.

3 Sift in the icing sugar and beat together until smooth but still firm.

4 Using a tablespoon, fold in the biscuit crumbs. Use immediately or store in the refrigerator for up to 2–3 days.

Glacé Icing

Makes enough to cover 12 whoopies
175 g/6 oz icing sugar
5–6 tsp hot water

1 Sift the icing sugar into a bowl. Add the hot water and stir until the mixture is smooth and thick enough to coat the back of a wooden spoon. Use immediately and leave to set.

VARIATIONS
Chocolate Glacé Icing
Replace 3 tablespoons of the icing sugar with 3 tablespoons cocoa powder.

Coffee Glacé Icing
Dissolve 1 tablespoon instant coffee in 1 tablespoon boiling water. Leave to cool and then mix with the icing sugar in place of the water, adding a little extra water, if necessary.

Mocha Glacé Icing
Replace 3 tablespoons of the icing sugar with 3 tablespoons cocoa powder. Dissolve 2 teaspoons instant coffee in 1 tablespoon boiling water. Leave to cool and then mix with the icing sugar in place of the water, adding a little extra water, if necessary.

Coloured Glacé Icing
Using paste or liquid food colouring of your choice, such as red, green or yellow, dip the tip of a skewer into the colouring, add to the icing and stir until evenly coloured to the shade that you want.

Orange or Lemon Glacé Icing
Replace the water with orange or lemon juice, and colour with orange or yellow food colouring, as in Coloured Glacé Icing, if you wish.

Chocolate Ganache

Makes enough to cover 12 whoopies
150 g/5½ oz plain chocolate
150 ml/5 fl oz double cream
small knob of butter

1 Break the chocolate into a heatproof bowl and add the cream. Stand the bowl over a saucepan of simmering water and heat until the chocolate has melted, stirring constantly.

2 Remove from the heat and add the butter. Stir until smooth and shiny. Leave to cool for about 2 hours, stirring occasionally, until firm enough to spread. Store in the refrigerator for up to 2–3 days and return to room temperature before using.

Party Decorating Ideas

Children's Birthday Whoopies

Bake a batch of Chocolate or Vanilla Whoopies. Fill with Chocolate Buttercream. Cover with Chocolate or Coloured Glacé Icing and leave to set. Dust with cake sprinkles and add a candle to each.

Children's Party Box

Bake a batch of Chocolate Whoopies. Fill with Chocolate Buttercream. Cover with Chocolate Glacé Icing. Sprinkle with candy-coated chocolate sweets and leave to set. Pack individually in a box to take home.

After-Dinner Whoopies

Bake a batch of Mini Chocolate Whoopies. Spread the bottom halves with Chocolate Buttercream. Cover the top halves with Chocolate Ganache, put on top of the bottom halves and leave to set. Put the filled whoopies in a small dish to serve.

Host & Hostess Whoopies

Bake a batch of Mini Vanilla Whoopies. Spread the bottom halves with Chocolate Buttercream or Chocolate Marshmallow Crème. Cover the top halves with Chocolate Ganache, put on top of the bottom halves and leave to set. Pack in a box to give as a gift.

Valentine Whoopies

Make for an engagement party or any other romantic celebration. Bake a batch of Red Velvet Whoopies (see page 22). Using a heart-shape cutter, cut into hearts. Fill with Vanilla Buttercream, Classic Marshmallow Filling or Home-made Marshmallow Crème. Cover with Glacé Icing, decorate with large heart-shaped cake sprinkles and leave to set. Pack in a box to give as a gift.

Wedding Whoopies

Bake a batch of Mini Vanilla Whoopies. Fill with Vanilla Buttercream, Classic Marshmallow Filling or Home-made Marshmallow Crème. Cover with white Glacé Icing, add pink sugar flower cake decorations and leave to set. If you wish, spray with pink edible lustre spray. Put in a dish to serve.

Silver or Gold Anniversary Whoopies

Bake a batch of Mini Vanilla Whoopies. Fill with Vanilla Buttercream, Classic Marshmallow Filling or Home-made Marshmallow Crème. Cover with white Glacé Icing, add silver or gold dragees (cake decoration balls) and leave to set. If you wish, spray with silver or gold edible lustre spray. Put in a dish to serve.

Baby Shower Whoopies

Bake a batch of Mini Vanilla Whoopies. Fill with Vanilla Buttercream, Classic Marshmallow Filling or Home-made Marshmallow Crème. Cover half with pale pink and half with pale blue Glacé Icing. Put a pink, blue or white sugared almond on top of each and leave to set. Put in a dish to serve.

Easter Whoopies

Bake a batch of Mini Chocolate Whoopies. Fill with Chocolate Buttercream. Cover with Chocolate Glacé Icing, put a mini chocolate Easter egg on top of each and leave to set. To serve, pile in a basket filled with tissue paper or shredded coloured paper. Alternatively, don't ice the whoopies but add a mini chocolate Easter egg and wrap in coloured foil. Hide in the garden or house and have an Easter whoopie treasure hunt.

Halloween Whoopies

Bake a batch of Pumpkin Whoopies (see page 44). Fill with orange Coloured Buttercream. Cover with orange Coloured Glacé Icing and leave to set. Add a Halloween cake decoration to each before serving in a dish.

Christmas Whoopies

Bake a batch of Mini Vanilla Whoopies. Fill with Vanilla Buttercream, Classic Marshmallow Filling or Home-made Marshmallow Crème. Cut out star shapes from ready-rolled white fondant icing to fit the tops of the whoopies. Place on top of each and decorate with silver or gold dragees (cake decoration balls). Pack into cellophane bags and tie with ribbon to give as gifts.

Up-a-Notch Decorating Ideas

For Adults & the Young at Heart

Bake a batch of Chocolate or Vanilla Whoopies. Fill with Buttercream and roll the sides in chopped pistachio nuts, flaked almonds, chopped pecan nuts, chopped walnuts or cocoa powder.

Top with a piped swirl of Buttercream and add fresh fruit such as a strawberry or raspberry, or a small chocolate.

For Children

Bake a batch of Chocolate or Vanilla Whoopies, fill and then roll the sides in mini coloured candy-coated chocolates, chocolate chips, crushed sweets or cake-decorating sprinkles.

Top with a piped swirl of Buttercream and add a small chocolate, chocolate buttons or a sweet.

Marbled Whoopies

Make a batch of Chocolate and a batch of Vanilla Whoopie mixture. Add the Vanilla Whoopie mixture to the Chocolate Whoopie mixture and, using a tablespoon, gently swirl the mixtures together to create a marbled effect. Don't overmix. Using a level 5-cm/2-inch ice cream scoop or heaped tablespoon, put the mixture onto baking paper-lined baking sheets in 5-cm/2-inch diameter rounds about 3 cm/1¼ inches high, leaving at least 7.5 cm/3 inches between each round to allow room for spreading. Alternatively, put the mixture in a greased whoopie pan. The mixture will make 24 whoopies. Fill with Chocolate or Vanilla Buttercream, or Home-made Marshmallow Crème or Chocolate Marshmallow Crème.

Chocolate-coated Whoopies

Make a batch of Chocolate Ganache. Take a filled Chocolate or Vanilla Whoopie or Mini Chocolate or Mini Vanilla Whoopie and dip half the whoopie in the warm Chocolate Ganache. Put on a wire rack, with a sheet of baking paper or a tray under the rack to catch the drips, and leave to set.

Black & White Whoopies

Bake a batch of Chocolate Whoopies and a batch of Vanilla Whoopies and match each 'black' whoopie half with its closest 'white' partner in size. This will make 24 whoopies. Fill with Chocolate or Vanilla Buttercream, or Home-made Marshmallow Crème or Chocolate Marshmallow Crème, or add a layer of both.

Packaging & Presentation Ideas

The traditional way to wrap whoopies is in clingfilm. This is not only a good way to store them but also makes them portable. They will keep like this at room temperature for up to three days.

To give as a gift, pack in cellophane bags, stacking them with a square of baking paper between them to prevent them from sticking together. Tie with ribbon and add a tag.

Large whoopies can be arranged on a decorative plate and the whole thing wrapped in cellophane, tied with ribbon and given as a gift along with the plate.

Pack Mini Whoopies in a single layer in an airtight container or box. If not iced, they can be individually tied with thin ribbon to make them look attractive.

A gift of home-made whoopies is always appreciated, and packed in a stylish box, they will be especially welcomed. Boxes are easy to make and you will gain as much satisfaction from creating them as the person will from receiving the whoopie. Sample templates are provided on the following pages. Line the box with tissue paper or baking paper before filling with whoopies, placing baking paper between them if stacking.

A box for 1 whoopie

All of the templates are printed at half size. The template on this page can be photocopied at 200% scale. The other templates should be copied onto thin card using the measurements provided.

To make the boxes, carefully cut as marked. Use a butter knife and a straightedge rule to score along the fold marks, then stick down the corners with a little white (PVA) glue, being careful not to let any glue get on to the exposed surfaces. Leave the glue to dry completely before you use the box.

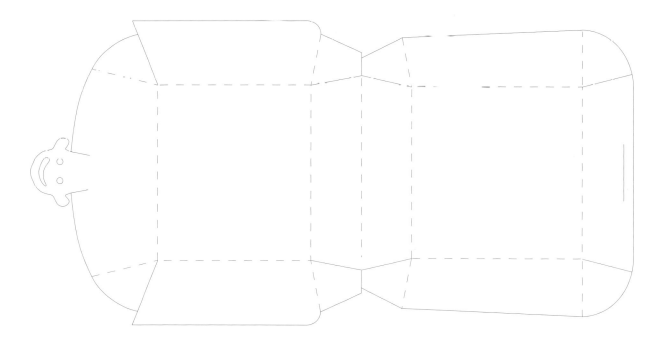

—————— Cut

– – – – – Fold

A box for 6 mini whoopies

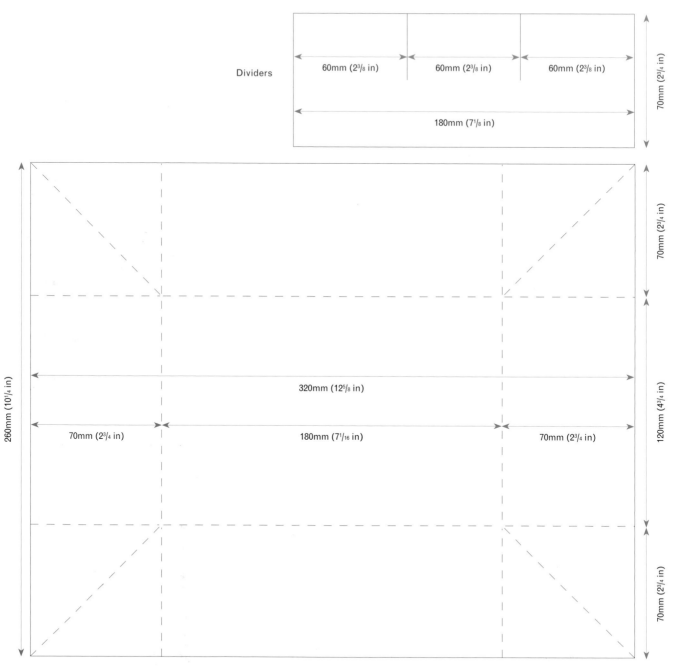

Dividers

60mm (2³/₈ in)   60mm (2³/₈ in)   60mm (2³/₈ in)

70mm (2³/₄ in)

180mm (7¹/₈ in)

70mm (2³/₄ in)

320mm (12⁵/₈ in)

120mm (4³/₄ in)

260mm (10¹/₄ in)

70mm (2³/₄ in)   180mm (7¹/₁₆ in)   70mm (2³/₄ in)

70mm (2³/₄ in)

Bottom

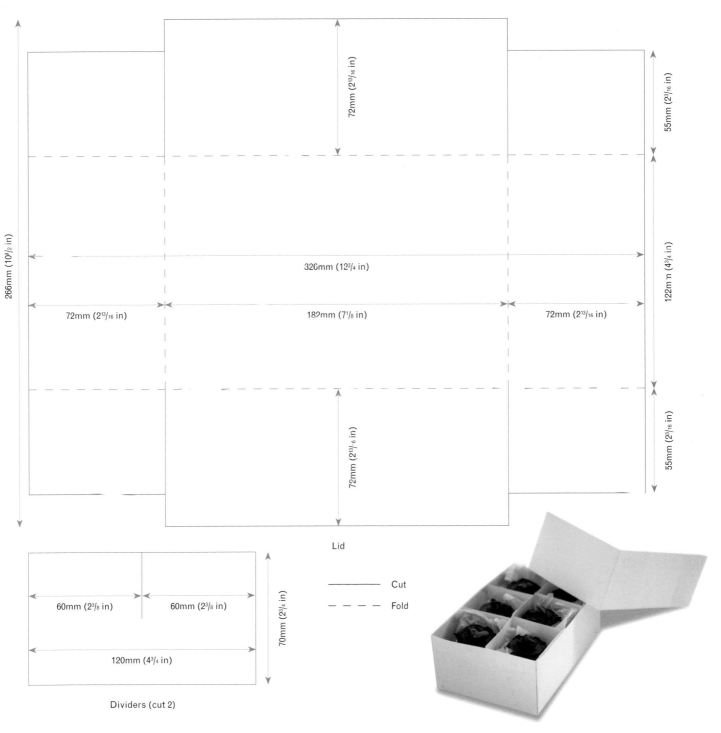

266mm (10¹/₂ in)

72mm (2¹³/₁₆ in)

55mm (2³/₁₆ in)

326mm (12³/₄ in)

122mm (4³/₄ in)

72mm (2¹³/₁₆ in)

182mm (7¹/₈ in)

72mm (2¹³/₁₆ in)

72mm (2¹³/₁₆ in)

55mm (2³/₁₆ in)

Lid

60mm (2³/₈ in)

60mm (2³/₈ in)

70mm (2³/₄ in)

120mm (4³/₄ in)

Dividers (cut 2)

Cut

Fold

A box for
4 whoopies

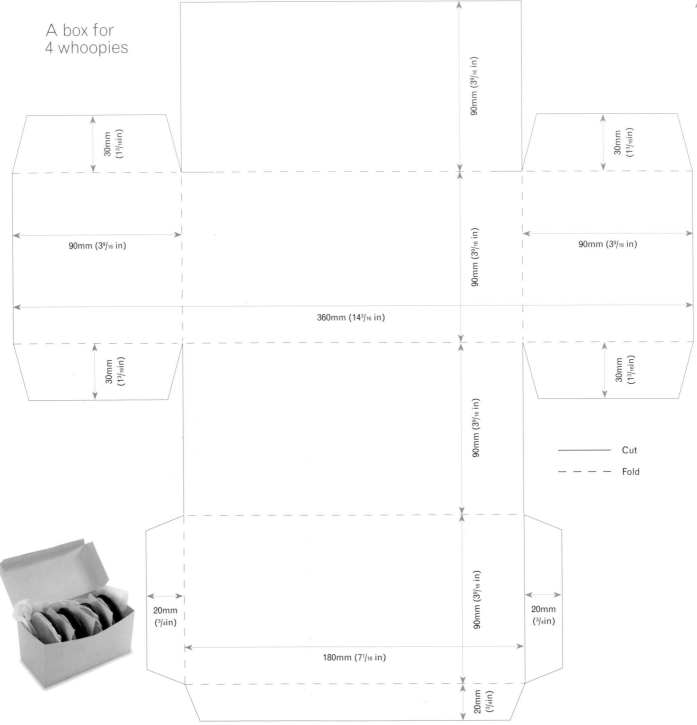

30mm (1³/₁₆ in)

90mm (3⁹/₁₆ in)

90mm (3⁹/₁₆ in)

30mm (1³/₁₆ in)

30mm (1³/₁₆in)

90mm (3⁹/₁₆ in)

90mm (3⁹/₁₆ in)

30mm (1³/₁₆in)

360mm (14³/₁₆ in)

380mm (14¹⁵/₁₆ in)

——————— Cut

– – – – – Fold

90mm (3⁹/₁₆ in)

20mm (³/₄in)

90mm (3⁹/₁₆ in)

20mm (³/₄in)

180mm (7¹/₁₆ in)

20mm (³/₄in)

Index

Published in 2011 by New Holland Publishers (UK) Ltd

London • Cape Town • Sydney • Auckland
www.newhollandpublishers.com

Garfield House, 86–88 Edgware Road,
London W2 2EA, United Kingdom

80 McKenzie Street, Cape Town 8001,
South Africa

Unit 1, 66 Gibbes Street, Chatswood,
NSW 2067, Australia

218 Lake Road, Northcote,
Auckland, New Zealand

10 9 8 7 6 5 4 3 2 1

A catalogue record for this book is available from the British Library

ISBN: 978-1-84773-927-8

Printed in China

This book was conceived, designed, and produced by

Ivy Press
210 High Street, Lewes
East Sussex BN7 2NS, UK
www.ivy-group.co.uk

Creative Director Peter Bridgewater
Publisher Jason Hook
Editorial Director Tom Kitch
Senior Designer James Lawrence
Designer Ginny Zeal
Editor Jo Richardson
Photographer Jeremy Hopley
Stylist Susanna Tee

Acknowledgments
The publisher would like to thank the Steamer Trading Cookshop
(20/21 High Street, Lewes, UK) for providing the props for the
photoshoot, and iStockphoto/Kathleen Spencer for permission to
reproduce copyright material on page 67.